T0113550

A LIFE-LONG COMMITMENT TO CHANGE: BEGINNING WITH THE END IN MIND

A LIFE-LONG COMMITMENT TO CHANGE: BEGINNING WITH THE END IN MIND

DR. VICTORIA C. TAYLOR

Archway Publishing books may be ordered through booksellers or by contacting:

Archway Publishing
1663 Liberty Drive
Bloomington, IN 47403
www.archwaypublishing.com
844-669-3957

Because of the dynamic nature of the Internet, any web addresses or links contained in this book may have changed since publication and may no longer be valid. The views expressed in this work are solely those of the author and do not necessarily reflect the views of the publisher, and the publisher hereby disclaims any responsibility for them.

ISBN: 978-1-6657-4570-3 (sc)
ISBN: 978-1-6657-4571-0 (e)

Library of Congress Control Number: 2023911273

Print information available on the last page.

Archway Publishing rev. date: 06/16/2023

CONTENTS

DEDICATION

This short, five-chapter book, "A Lifelong Commitment to Change: Beginning with the End in Mind", was written for my parents (Denise Johnson and Ronald Whiting, Sr.), my husband (i.e., my KING), Lionel F. Taylor, II, and my siblings, Ronald, Jr., Veronica, Joseph, Daniel, Ronnese, Kiarra, Debra, Karen, Ophelia, and Aaron. Your deserved affirmations hold a special place in my mind and heart. It is time to fly! Share your passions and talents with the world! Our children will observe us and then create their own journeys.

Also, I dedicate this book to *every* learner who enrolls in any psychology course I teach at Prince George's Community College (PGCC); it is my full intention to do the following: challenge you intellectually, motivate you extrinsically, encourage you to develop intrinsic motivation to excel in my course, share knowledge, facilitate skills development and practice, extend a networking opportunity that involves communicating with academic librarians, provide help and support, and hold you accountable. Why? Two reasons. First, I am a proud PGCC alum, and it is one of my goals to give back to the place where it all began for me, academically. Second, challenges can bring out the best in us!

FOREWORD

After intense moments of reflection, it was decided that even if this book only helps one person see their fullest potential can only be unlocked by them, I have at least paid forward a small slither of what was shared with me over the years. Let me begin by unpacking the title and sharing the meaning behind it. A life-long commitment to change requires an openness to new experiences and a deep-rooted belief in oneself to be able to shine, despite the challenges, obstacles, and even threats that may come your way. Change can be perceived as good, bad, or indifferent but perception is fleeting. We change and adapt every day, ebbing and flowing with what life throws our way. Yet, it is chiefly not until one has been asked or told to change course that change becomes the enemy. I get it. Change can be extremely uncomfortable, even scary, but it can also be extremely rewarding.

One month before my 30th birthday, a decision was made to never settle and always strive for what is in my best interest. Beginning with the end in mind, I figured I had at least another 30 to 50 years of life to live. My thinking was what I did then would shape what life looks like now. It turned out to be true. What did that decision require? That decision required I grab the bull by the horns and steer it in the direction I wanted to go, and that direction was upward and onward.

This is not a how to or self-help type of book, and it is also not an autobiography depicting the chronicles of my life. Instead, it is a, short, chapter formatted book, meant to highlight how a lifetime commitment to change, beginning with the end in mind, will keep you in the game—the game of life that comes with no instructions but many rules, regulations, policies, and laws.

Chapter 1—forecasting the future—is about assessing your current situation right before making this lifelong commitment to change. Chapter 2—seeking and finding necessary human, social, and financial capital for success—is about situating yourself among others who are more experienced, resourceful, and genuinely interested in opening a door for you to *walk* into or a window for you to *climb* into. Chapter 3—making a lifelong commitment to change—is about envisioning the future you see for yourself and digging your heels in, knowing you may have to adapt, rethink, or change course along the way to achieve what success looks like for you. Chapter 4—moving the goal posts on purpose with purpose—is about satisfying the whole you, physically, mentally, socially, and emotionally, as you grow through your accomplishments and setbacks; you are not the same you five or ten years down the road, and goals change. Last, Chapter 5—legacy building and torch passing—is about leading by example and paying forward the blessings of a steady paced race; the blessings that keep on giving include sharing knowledge, resources, and access, modeling an example of how to soar upward and onward, and planting seeds that eventually lead to a garden full of the next generation of beautiful, bright, and unapologetically bold leaders.

There are many paths to success and rarely do we get on one road and keep straight to our destination. A life-long commitment to change is equivalent to a life-long commitment to learning. If you can imagine where you want to go or be in life, take it a step further and execute a plan of action that will get you there, recognizing at the onset that the road there may become winding and uphill. When challenges or threats arise find a way around it, under it, over it, or through it if you must, but stay the course even when the course temporarily appears unrecognizable. Everybody's journey is different, but to get anywhere you first must *begin* the journey.

Here are a few questions that should be asked in cycles or waves as you dig into what this book has to offer. Who am I? What do I want to accomplish? How badly do I want it? What must I do to achieve it? I recall asking myself these questions as a teenager approaching early adulthood, again in the latter half of my early adulthood years, and now again, as Dr. Victoria C. Taylor, who is currently in the first half of middle adulthood. The point is, once you answer these questions for yourself, act! Take the necessary steps to bring to fruition the vision you have envisioned for yourself; you can remain idle or strive to be an idol, but you must believe the choice is yours to make.

With over ten years of qualitative research experience and expertise in behavioral health research, a conscious decision was made to write this nonfiction novel using a storytelling approach. There is power in storytelling, for the person telling the story, the person receiving the story, and all those who become influenced because a connection was established. I do not aim to predict what that connection may be, but sometimes a single spark is all it takes to light something/ someone on fire. Maybe it is the thought that if this person can do this, so can I. This is the goal, ultimately—to bring *your attention* to what is *your desire in life* and how do *you achieve it*. I do not provide the answers to your questions, but if you are developing questions and beginning to seek resolutions, I have done my part.

CHAPTER ONE
FORECASTING THE FUTURE

Forecasting the Future

Here is what I learned about fifteen years ago. I was alive and grateful for it, but I knew I wasn't living my best life. Did I have a job with a decent salary, a vehicle, a roof over my head, a man, nice clothes, shoes, purses, jewelry, and the freedom to travel where I liked when I liked because I had no children? Yes, across the board. To somebody this could sound like living your best life. I wasn't struggling by any stretch of the imagination, but I wasn't happy, recognizing happiness is subjective. Material things can be replaced in many instances. I knew I had been in a whirlwind cycle to nowhere for 10 years, personally, professionally, and socially, and enough was enough! My twenties are a novel itself—a future thought (seed planted).

Sometimes we must make hard decisions. As I mentioned, and you will quickly come to learn the repeated patterns or messages throughout the book, change is hard and can be scary, but it can also be extremely rewarding. Here is what I know now; a life-long commitment to change requires you to commit to the changes unfolding. Sometimes the changes we commit to unfold, and come to fruition in relatively short order, and other times, it may require we buckle in for the long ride ahead.

When I was assessing my life's circumstances at the time, in 2006, I had reached a point of no return with moving forward or upward from my current situation. I was not subtle nor apologetic for my decision. I surrounded myself with people who also wanted to see me succeed and achieve the goals I set for myself. I learned quickly that was a fixed necessity and quite candidly, intentionally, I kept a small personal circle, but sought out an expansive academic turned professional circle. I will delve more deeply into seeking and finding the necessary human and social capital for success in chapter two. In this chapter, the focus is more on how personality plays a role, among a host of other factors, in why we think what we think, do what we do, and feel what we feel.

What was I thinking? What was I doing? What was I feeling? These were the driving questions behind my decision to change lanes in my life. My head was not on straight for starters. I've always been game for intellectual challenges, even welcomed it, cross-training in most jobs I had held, but I was not making the smartest personal life decisions. Again, this is not a book where I will unleash my personal past, but I knew I was smarter than what I was revealing. My actions, frankly, matched my not so smart personal life decisions. Essentially, I felt like I was on a never-ending rollercoaster ride of the same, with no end in sight. If you can picture this with your own mind's eye, you can probably imagine quite a few scenarios. The point is sometimes we must reach that point within that burst out, and when it does, freedom has a new meaning. I was thinking differently. My actions matched my new way of seeing life, and my emotions were usually aligned with my experiences. Yet, what was most important was that I found and maintained a new balance in life.

This brings me to a conversation, though relatively brief, about personality. It is one of the contributing factors that can explain why you think, behave, and feel the way you do about life's experiences. I will not get into theories here, but I will say our personalities form relatively early in life and they typically remain steadfast. Our personality reflects who we are as a person, but I must acknowledge our environment and the people in it influence our personality as well.

I am offering a single testament about personality. I have had the same strong-willed, unbreakable, steadfast, personality for as long as I can recall. Seriously! Does it sometimes get me in trouble? Yes. Has it also gotten me through whatever life has thrown my way? Absolutely! Your personality is how you would describe to someone who you are and descriptives of how you present yourself or how you believe others see you. One's personality is typically the same from a very young age into late adulthood. Who you are when you are young becomes more solidified and resilient as you age. For instance, when someone says, "oh, don't expect them to change they are stuck in their way," what they are saying is that person has been that way all their life because that is who they are. The other amazing thing about personality is that everyone is unique and has their own personality, including identical twins even when similarities exist. Usually, if someone is asked to describe their personality, they will rattle off a list of adjectives (e.g., words or phrases that describe you). I will present a brief list and the main takeaway is that how I decide to present myself at any given moment is context specific—in that moment with that person or those persons is why I have decided to present myself in whatever manner for a reason. I am beautiful, bold, brave, calculated, candid, caring, easing going, educated, faithful, funny (in my opinion), happy, honest, humbled, objective, open-minded, passionate, protective about who and what I love, reasonable, rebellious, when necessary, resilient, secure, sensitive, scientific, strong-willed, tactful, talented, teachable, well-rounded, and well-travelled. This is who I am, and I am always ready for whatever comes my way.

Change—for the better—has always been a part of my success equation. I find it hard to understand, sometimes, when I observe the amount of effort exerted into pushing back on change. I have intentionally learned the distinction between change for the better and change for the worse. No one should welcome change for the worse; the notion suggests that would be counterproductive. Yet, to be clear, change for the better does not exclude failure; failure too is part of the success equation. Simply put, if you have never failed, how do you recognize success?

Some may push back at the previous question and travel down the road of some people are born into a set path for success. My counter is simple and straightforward. It is nonsensical to assume individual people are guaranteed to be successful simply because the generations before them have shown or told them how they have succeeded. It is also nonsensical to assume the opposite being those who have come from generations of repeated failure just are not meant to succeed. You can get thousands of "no" responses before getting that one "yes" response that can change your life for the better, maybe even forever.

This brings me to the main point of this chapter, forecasting the future. How do you do this, you might be wondering? Surely, I had no magical ball, but I did have a plan. Forecasting the future requires you to think backwards from the place of success you envision for yourself. What? I will use my journey to becoming Dr. Victoria C. Taylor, maiden name, Johnson, as one example of a lifelong commitment to change, that required executing the plan—accepting and adapting to change along the way. What I understood from the onset is that the goal posts would continuously move. I accepted that expectation right from the start.

As a nontraditional, first generation, minority female student walking through the doors of Prince George's Community College (PGCC) for the first time, I knew this would be the first step in the academic journey. It was the most financially feasible decision to start at a community college, but at age 30, at the time, I didn't have any time to spare. What I knew walking in the door was that my mission was to tell the stories of the underrepresented and underserved and find ways to help them. I thought it would be via the route of majoring in English or mass communication with a concentration in journalism. What I was seeking to explore, better understand, and find ways to help—being minority health disparities—could all be discovered in the world of psychology. This became apparent to me halfway through my General Psychology course taught by Dr. Janice Armstrong at PGCC, during the fall 2006 semester—my second semester as a part-time college student and full-time employee at a law firm in DC. My commitment at that moment became actualized in my mind; so much so that I began the process of researching what would the entire academic journey look like if I wanted a career in the discipline of psychology. Right away I knew at a minimum I would have to earn my master's degree in psychology, and likely would require a doctorate if I wanted to excel. This is exactly what I mean by working backwards. I set the goal. I inquired about what would need to be accomplished to achieve the goal. Then, I set a plan in motion knowing it would be years before my destination would be reached. What mattered the most was that I was determined to succeed no matter what life threw my way—challenges or threats. I would find a way around it, over it, under it, or through it, if I must. Quitting was not an option—period.

With that said, the very next semester, I was faced with a series of serious challenges that required a temporary year-long pause, but as I stated quitting was not an option. For me it is my faith, family (born into, married into, and created), then everyone and everything else. The year 2007 was a test of my determination, strength, and willpower. I had the first of many major surgeries, was informed I would likely not be able to successfully give birth, and my mom and siblings had become homeless. Yet, I was resolved on restarting my academic journey, getting my family through the challenge of homelessness, and improving my overall work-academic-life situation. By 2008, the first mission was accomplished. My siblings and mom were all back together again, and I was re-enrolled at PGCC. In fact, not only had I re-enrolled, but I had been doing my research all along on how to make my dreams a reality and was awarded a scholarship that would cover my tuition and fees for the remainder of my academic journey at PGCC. This scholarship program was a pipeline program whereby the agreement was to transfer to the University of Maryland at College Park (UMCP) after graduating from PGCC. It was formerly called the Hillman Entrepreneurs Program and is now named the Southern Management Leadership Program transferring from PGCC and Montgomery College to UMCP. Again, I was making decisions and moves with the end game in mind.

I would no longer have to figure out what four-year college I would get accepted into or transfer to after earning my associate degree. With the financial hurdle jumped, my focus turned to making myself known and putting my existing knowledge and skills to use (ex-military: Army, radio station administrator: WINA, WKAV & WQMZ, medical malpractice law office & engineering firm receptionist, and patent law cross-trained legal clerk). Therefore, I returned in January of 2008 (spring semester) ready to hit the ground running. I shared my interests and goals with the program director, at the time, of the Hillman Entrepreneurs Program at PGCC, Ms. Lisa Rawlings. I had no idea then, that she would be the Heaven-sent spark that changed my life forever, for the better. Ms. Rawlings introduced me to Professor Sonia Bell, my lifelong mentor turned colleague and friend. From that relationship, the door was opened, and I was invited into the research arena. That fire has burned ever so brightly ever since.

I had discovered how I could leverage my prior knowledge and accumulation of skills. I delved into the world of research and created my own path through undergraduate and graduate school. Beginning fall 2008, research became a constant in my academic career. I conducted research as an independent learner for credit and only had to report to Professor Sonia Bell incrementally across the semester because she was confident that I was working with minimal guidance. I presented a scientific poster at Johns Hopkins in the fall of 2008, also thanks to Professor Sonia Bell. I applied for and was awarded a paid summer research internship every summer following while in undergrad [summer 2009: University of California San Francisco (UCSF)—last year at PGCC; summer 2010: University of California Los Angeles (UCLA)—first year at UMD at College Park]. I was actively engaged in two research labs while enrolled at UMCP: a graduate level counseling psychology lab, and a graduate level evolutionary biology lab. Tying this all into forecasting the future is quite simple and straightforward. I knew this journey, at a minimum, would be six years, and once the decision was made that I would not stop until I earned my doctorate degree, I knew I could easily be adding an additional seven years to the clock before reaching completion. I accepted this challenge welcomingly.

I mapped out a fifteen-year plan. The questions became focused on where I see myself in fifteen years—not five years. I was thinking about the long haul rather than the incremental steps along the way. I knew I would need to be able to demonstrate what is expected in graduate school and that was the rationale for jumping into the fire. My introduction to research could be characterized as "baptism by fire" because as an independent learner, I was given a charge and a timeline, and the rest was on me, again, with some guidance, advice, and lots of constructive feedback. The point is, I showed up and have been showing out ever since. I have never been a fan of the saying, faking it until you make it, nor do I struggle with imposter syndrome. I am comfortable with who I am and the skin I live in. I am wise enough to know I will never know everything but will always be open to learning something new.

To forecast the future, you must think about your current situation and develop a mental map that is layered. This will require you to be intrinsically motivated—the need to be motivated by your own personal desire to become the best you that you can be in this lifetime. Extrinsic motivation like money and status has its limits, in my opinion. If you are not internally driven to achieve the goals you set for yourself, incentives will not have a long-lasting effect. This brings me to the point of digging your heels in. You will need to establish strong roots. Think about a very wide and tall tree with hundreds of strong branches that has withstood the beatings of wind and water storms, repeatedly; that massive and strong tree started as a seed. The development of your mental map is planting the seed but just like the massive and strong tree after years of growth you must nourish it all along the way. Therefore, the remainder of this chapter will focus on the development of a mental map.

A mental map (Figure 1) is a structured process of developing new ideas/information/goals or organizing existing ideas/information/goals such that the bigger picture is broken down into meaningful but smaller size achievable parts. More importantly, mental maps provide a very expansive and flexible approach to thinking through new or old ideas/information/goals. At the onset of this journey when establishing this layered mental map, I did not know in advance all the institutions I would go on to attend.

Figure 1

Mental Map

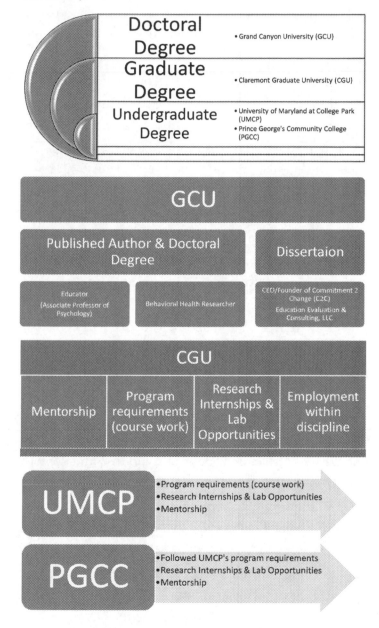

What I did know from the start is that I would not quit until the highest level of education had been achieved. I had no desire to reach an invisible ceiling. The overlapping and continuous part that showed up at every level was research. The only reason I am highlighting this point is because it is important in all disciplines, but especially important for evidence-based practices. Your mental map, of course, should include your ideas/information/goals that have been broken down into those smaller, meaningful parts that can be achieved over time. What will your mental map look like and what will you do to start moving toward your destiny?

Again, you must do this with the end game always at the fore-front of your mind. It has never been about where one starts, but it has always been about where one ends because of the decisions made in life. What decisions will you make today? Will you welcome the changes that result from your decision-making? Will you nourish the seeds you plant and then watch them grow?

To be clear, your mental map does not have to be elaborate. It needs to be sensible, organized, and always in your face. My mental maps lived on my refrigerator, bathroom mirror, and taped inside of the front cover of my day calendar. All places that ensured I would have to see it every day. It is a necessity because there is nothing worse, in my opinion, than knowing what you believe you deserve in this lifetime, that we only get one opportunity to live, and do nothing to bring it to fruition. We are in control of our own destinies no mat-ter the expectations or limitations inflicted upon us. This is a very important point to end with because your dreams can live and die in your head before you ever make a move. The purpose, again, of this chapter, is to bring your focus on you. How resilient are you when challenges and threats come your way? How steadfast do you become after developing a plan/goal; do you execute the plan after putting so much thought and effort into its creation?

Where you perceive yourself to be in life, right now, is always relative—to the comparison of others because we are social beings. Keep in mind that once you decide for yourself where you are in life, where you desire to be in life, and what you are going to do about it to bring it to fruition, *a commitment to those changes that will come* is a precondition of the journey.

CHAPTER TWO

SEEKING AND FINDING NECESSARY HUMAN, SOCIAL, AND FINANCIAL CAPITAL FOR SUCCESS

Seeking and Finding Necessary Human, Social, and Financial Capital for Success

Once the journey has been planned out, it is time to execute it. Procrastination has killed many dreams, goals, and aspirations. Do not fall into that trap. Remember, it is perfectly fine to take it one day at a time. Sometimes, it is one hour, or minute, or one step at a time. Whichever the case, forward and upward is the direction to strive for because nothing worth having is usually easily attained. You must work for it. Make it happen. Create what you desire if it does not exist. Yet, with an abundance of intrinsic motivation and drive to thrive, you will still need to surround yourself with individuals who genuinely want to see you succeed as well. Sometimes the individuals you need in your expansive professional or academic circle may only have one purpose to serve, and other times there may be individuals who play an intricate role in coaching, guiding, and modeling what needs to be learned, understood, and put into practice. This brings the focus of the story now to seeking out and finding the necessary human, social, and financial capital that will be needed to fuel and sustain your success.

Whether you are in middle school, high school, college, or already working in your field, discipline, or area of interest, it is critical that you create a support system that will push you beyond your doubts and fears. Typically, if you are experiencing doubts or fears you have been challenged in some way. Here is what I know about challenges. Just like a threat, it can cripple you and trigger a fight or flight response. However, challenges can bring out the best in us—our "A" game. Make us step up. A challenge, for example, is getting told "no" time and time, again, when trying to attain the goal(s) you have set in motion. Yet, the "no" responses serve as learning opportunities because it only takes that one "yes" response to soar, perhaps even beyond your wildest dreams.

Who needs to be in your ark? I will start by saying who should not be in your ark. Keep out those who are piercing small holes every time they appear. That is all I will say about that because it is more important to focus on what you are in control of rather than what you cannot control—being others. Once you determine your initial destiny, you need to do your research. We learn to do our homework as early as Pre-K in our grading system. It should not be surprising I am telling you to do your homework; it never stops. Ask yourself the hard and necessary questions. What will it take to achieve the goal I've set for myself? This will likely include people, finances, and other non-monetary resources. I will give examples of other non-monetary (social) resources, but first understand this journey cannot be travelled alone. You will need people in your ark that are there for a sole purpose as well as those who are there to guide you along the journey.

Who are these people? We can start with the supernatural, no matter your religion, faith, traditions, or practices. I choose to use the term supernatural because who or what I am referring to is not present in the human flesh. Faith or belief, even the size of a tiny mustard seed, is critical to withstand all the challenges or threats that life may throw your way. There is research that supports the hypothesis that religion or faith and associated practices are related to increased happiness, especially as we age. Next, *you* must show up prepared to give all you got to accomplish the goal(s) you have set for yourself, recognizing striving for perfection is great, but usually unrealistic. Make sure you are setting SMART goals—Specific, Measurable, Attainable, Realistic, and Timely (SMART). Be the person that attracts those who have the means and want to open doors or windows for you to get a little closer to achieving your goal(s); do not allow an unnecessary goal of perfection to push people away or make people shut doors you desire to enter. If you come across as knowing everything you need to know and nothing you do or have done can be wrong, it will likely turn off or away the people I am going to move on to now.

From the moment the decision is made to achieve the goal(s) set, you will need people in your ark that have the knowledge, skills, resources or access to resources, and willingness to help and support *you* in building the strongest ark possible. Sometimes these are people who share beneficial knowledge or information with you and other times these are people willing and ready to guide, coach, and mentor you throughout the journey—academic or professional.

Those who are willing and ready to open the doors or windows that will enable a step in your success journey are equitable mentors/coaches/guides. These are seasoned people in your area of interest, academically or professionally, who genuinely want to help you achieve your goals, recognizing soon you will likely become their peer or near equal. These will be the people helping to strengthen your ark and repair the holes pierced by those bringing doubt or disdain secretly, or blatantly with every appearance. Equitable mentors are those who will not view you as a competitor but instead as an asset to the team soon.

A small sample of chiefly, non-traditional, four-year college graduates, from a pipeline entrepreneurship program that began at a community college, described the significance of *equitable entrepreneurial mentoring relationships* as being central to the success achieved during their academic journey. As one example of how important it is to have the right people in your academic or professional circle, "the category identified as equitable entrepreneurial mentoring relationships, served as the bedrock, foundation, or springboard for all the other categories to be possible" (Taylor, 2022, p. 145). Those other categories believed to be possible because of the mentoring relationships established included: skills development, help and support, networking opportunities, and attitudes toward quitting (Taylor, 2022; Figure 2). Even though these are the results of a qualitative, descriptive design (QDD) study with a small sample size (N=11; 11 participants), the takeaway is that genuinely established mentoring/coaching/guiding relationships serve as part of the roots that ground you in your success journey.

Figure 2

Categories: Synthesis of Reduced Initial Repeated Codes

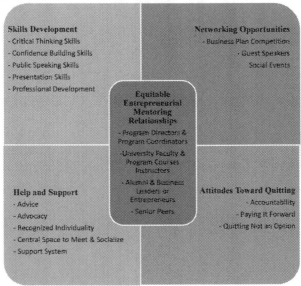

When you seek out human capital, ensuring they are the people genuinely interested in your success, you typically will come to find yourself wanting to become that mentor/coach/guide for others in the future. Human capital being part of social capital typically unlocks access to financial capital. The major takeaway is that human and social capital are fixed necessities in your lifelong journey.

Social capital refers to the value and benefits that come from the relationships, networks, and connections we have with other people in our society. It's like a form of currency that is based on trust, co-operation, and mutual support between individuals or groups/teams.

Think of it this way: Imagine you have a close friend who is always there for you when you need help or advice. This friend is well-connected and knows many other people who are willing to as-sist as well. In times of need, you can rely on your friend's network to provide resources, opportunities, or assistance. This is an example of social capital. Having social capital means having a strong network of relationships and connections that can be beneficial in various aspects of life. It can help you find job opportunities, get recommendations, access information, receive support during difficult times, and even enhance your overall well-being. The more robust your network and the stronger your relationships, the higher your social capital.

Just like financial capital (money) can be used to achieve goals or solve problems, social capital operates in a similar way. Social capital can be seen as a kind of resource that can be invested and utilized. When you have strong social capital, it means you have a network of people who you can rely on for support, advice, and opportunities. It provides you with resources and opportunities that you might not have access to on your own. By investing time and effort into building and nurturing relationships, you can increase your social capital and reap the rewards it brings.

Having social capital can bring various advantages. Building social capital involves investing time and effort in building and maintaining relationships, being active in communities, and being trustworthy and helpful to others. It's like building a network of connections that can benefit *both you and others* in the long run. In summary, social capital is the value we gain from the relationships and connections we have with other people. It provides us with support, opportunities, and resources, and it can be built through meaningful interactions and being part of communities. This expansive network leverages your financial capital.

Financial capital refers to the monetary resources, assets, and wealth that individuals, businesses, or organizations possess. Financial capital is associated with money, investments, savings, and any other financial assets that can be used to generate income, make purchases, or invest in various ventures. Financial capital is a fundamental component of the economic system and plays a crucial role in driving economic activities. It enables individuals, businesses, or organizations to engage in transactions, invest in projects, and pursue economic opportunities. Access to financial capital is essential for economic growth and development. It facilitates investment in productive activities, stimulates innovation, and helps drive economic progress at both the individual and societal levels.

Financial capital is important because it enables individuals, businesses, or organizations to make economic decisions and participate in economic activities. It provides the means to start businesses, fund projects, make purchases, and generate income. Financial capital can be used to invest in productive assets, such as machinery or technology, which can lead to increased productivity and economic growth. Access to financial capital is often a determining factor in the ability to pursue opportunities and achieve financial goals that you set for yourself. It allows individuals, businesses, or organizations to save for the future, build wealth, and have a buffer against unexpected expenses or economic downturns. Financial capital also plays a role in enabling individuals, businesses, or organizations to borrow money, whether through loans or credit, to fund investments or make purchases; loans and credit are indeed an option, but I would caution against reaching your goal in the red.

Tying this into a lifelong commitment to change whereby you start with the end in mind, human, social, and financial capital are all necessary ingredients to achieve success. You must consider all influencing factors when creating your plan of action for the goal(s) you set for yourself. This has been my understanding and experiences.

Building and sustaining the necessary human, social, and financial capital is indeed crucial for achieving success in any endeavor. Let's explore each of these elements in more detail and consider additional insights.

1. Human Capital: Human capital refers to the knowledge, skills, experiences, and attributes that individuals possess. It is the cumulative result of education, training, personal development, and practical experience. By continually investing in your human capital, you enhance your ability to adapt, learn, and contribute effectively to various areas of life.

    To build human capital, you can:

    •   Pursue lifelong learning: Embrace a growth mindset and actively seek out opportunities for self-improvement. This can include formal education, attending workshops, reading books, taking online courses, or acquiring new skills through hands-on experience.
    •   Develop expertise: Identify your strengths and passions and focus on honing your skills in those areas. Become

an expert by consistently practicing and refining your abilities. For example, as an educator, I must be able to conduct research and practice what I teach/preach in the classroom setting.

- Cultivate emotional intelligence: Strengthen your interpersonal skills, self-awareness, empathy, and resilience. These qualities are essential for building meaningful relationships and effectively navigating social dynamics.
- Foster creativity: Encourage a curious and innovative mindset, as creativity can provide unique solutions to challenges and open doors to new opportunities.
- Maintain physical and mental well-being: Take care of your health, manage stress, and strive for a balanced lifestyle. A healthy body and mind are foundational to optimizing your human capital.

2. Social Capital: Social capital refers to the networks, relationships, and connections you build with others. It encompasses trust, reciprocity, and support within your social circles, including family, friends, colleagues, mentors, and community.

To cultivate social capital, you can:

- Nurture relationships: Invest time and effort in building genuine connections with people who share your values and aspirations. Actively engage with others, show empathy, and be willing to offer support when needed.
- Seek mentors and role models: Look for individuals who have achieved success in areas you aspire to excel in. Mentors can provide guidance, support, and valuable insights based on their own experiences.

- Participate in communities: Join professional associations, clubs, volunteer organizations, or online communities that align with your interests and goals. Engaging with like-minded individuals can lead to collaborative opportunities and a broader network.
- Be a giver: Offer help, advice, and support to others without expecting immediate returns. By being generous and supportive, you establish yourself as a valuable member of your social network.

3. Financial Capital: Financial capital represents the financial resources you possess or have access to, including money, investments, assets, and credit. While financial capital is not the sole determinant of success, it does provide resources that can facilitate personal and professional endeavors.

To manage and grow your financial capital, you can:

- Set financial goals: Define short-term and long-term financial objectives that align with your overall life goals. Create a budget, track your expenses, and prioritize saving and investing.
- Develop financial literacy: Educate yourself about personal finance, investments, and wealth management. This knowledge will empower you to make informed decisions and leverage your financial resources effectively.
- Diversify income streams: Explore opportunities to diversify your sources of income, such as starting a side business, investing in stocks or real estate, or acquiring new skills that can lead to higher-paying job opportunities.

- Seek professional advice: Consult with financial advisors, accountants, or experts who can provide guidance on wealth management, tax planning, and investment strategies.
- Practice responsible financial habits: Maintain good financial hygiene by managing debt responsibly, paying bills on time, and saving for emergencies. A solid financial foundation provides stability and enables you to pursue opportunities without undue financial stress.

In summary, building and sustaining human, social, and financial capital are integral to achieving success.

Again, I will provide a single, relatively short testament to the significance of building and sustaining the necessary human, social, and financial capital you will need to succeed. As stated, I had made an early decision to commit to earning my doctoral degree, knowing it could easily be more than a decade before the goal would be achieved. Simultaneously, this meant I had committed to earning at least three or four degrees which turned out to be four degrees (i.e., associate degree, bachelor's degree, master's degree, and doctoral degree). I knew financially this would be a feat. Therefore, finding ways to finance my education was top of mind when developing my mental map and action plan. Equally as important was seeking out and finding mentors that could provide the insight, guidance, coaching, and support needed to make informed decisions as I embarked on this academic turned professional journey. As shown in Figure 2, the mentoring relationships I have established over the almost two decades, now, have "served as the bedrock, foundation, or springboard" to my successful endeavors (Taylor, 2022, p. 145).

In a very linear manner, here is what I did. When I returned to restart my academic journey at PGCC, I had applied for and was awarded a pipeline program scholarship. By the start of the second semester after returning to PGCC, I had started researching how to fully finance my four-year degree. I applied for and was awarded a merit-based full ride scholarship (i.e., Maryland Transfer Academic Excellence Scholarship) as well as the late Howard P. Rawlings Grant that put to rest another financial hurdle. The same was not true for my graduate and professional level degrees. I did not have a full ride fellowship, but I was awarded a 50% fellowship. This means loans were warranted, sought out, and granted to cover the remaining costs while in graduate school and during my doctoral studies.

While in graduate school in California, thousands of miles away from my hometown (DC), I had to get creative in how I would earn an income and cover the costs of my education and living expenses. I got a work-study position as a graduate assistant to the Dean of Students and worked for one of my professors as an evaluation consultant. In my role as an evaluation consultant, I was promoted to qualitative data co-coordinator assisting with the development of the code book. This means I had two part-time jobs and was enrolled at CGU full-time. This required being mindful of my time, responsibilities, duties, attitude, actions, and demonstration of high emotional as well as cognitive intelligence, always. Now, did the exploration of what the daytime beach scenes had to offer up and down the west coast take place? Was the nightlife of Los Angeles (L.A.) County and Orange County explored? Did I build new lifelong friendships outside of graduate school? Yes, across the board. The point is whatever decision you make it will be your responsibility to create a quality life balance, to include the many hats you wear. Again, quitting was not an option. Hence, I buckled in and created a life for myself in CA. I continued to expand my academic turned professional circle of mentors and colleagues all the while remaining in contact with previously established mentors. Graduate school was no walk in the park and being able to reach out and seek help or support was a matter of success or failure in the endeavor. Upon successfully completing graduate school, I can firmly state that I was ready for the challenges of a doctoral program and the pattern of surrounding myself with a strong support system was repeated as I worked through my doctoral studies.

The personal commitment to enduring the hard work, long days, and oftentimes, long nights is predominantly the reason I can proudly say I have earned the right to be recognized as Dr. Victoria C. Taylor, but the human, social, and financial capital I sought out and invested in is the reason I am confident this is just the beginning of my new journey in life. I will get to moving the goal posts on purpose with a purpose after I delve a little deeper into what it really means to make a commitment to change. It can be hard and scary but remember it can also be very rewarding and life altering for the better *if you are ready* to make the commitment.

CHAPTER THREE

MAKING A LIFELONG COMMITMENT TO CHANGE

Making a Lifelong Commitment to Change

M aking a lifelong commitment to change for the better is significant in personal growth, fulfillment, and overall well-being. It involves continuously striving to improve oneself, being open to learning new things (e.g., information or understanding), developing healthier habits, and achieving the personal goals you set. Here are several compelling reasons why making this commitment is crucial and what it will require to accomplish such a feat:

1. Continuous Personal Growth: Committing to lifelong change allows individuals to continually grow and evolve. It enables them to expand their knowledge, skills, and perspectives, fostering a deeper understanding of themselves and the world around them. By embracing change, individuals can adapt to new situations, overcome challenges, and unlock their full potential.

2. Improved Relationships: Personal growth through lifelong commitment to change positively impacts relationships. As individuals evolve, they gain better self-awareness, emotional intelligence, and communication skills. This leads to healthier and more meaningful connections with others, fostering stronger bonds, empathy, and understanding. Also recognizing relationships, such as mentoring relationships can run its cycle, but hopefully the person on the receiving end will take the torch and continue the service of mentoring others.

3. Enhanced Well-being: Committing to change for the better contributes to improved physical, mental, and emotional well-being. Adopting healthier habits such as regular exercise, balanced nutrition, and self-care practices can lead to increased energy levels, reduced stress, and better overall health. Additionally, addressing negative thought patterns and working on personal development can promote emotional resilience and a greater sense of fulfillment.

4. Increased Resilience: Life is filled with challenges and setbacks. A lifelong commitment to change cultivates resilience, enabling individuals to bounce back from adversity and maintain a positive outlook. By adopting a growth mindset and embracing change, individuals develop the skills and mindset necessary to navigate life's inevitable ups and downs with resilience, determination, and adaptability.

5. Achievement of Personal Goals: Lifelong commitment to change provides a framework for setting and achieving personal goals. By continuously striving for improvement, individuals can establish clear objectives, create action plans, and work towards their aspirations. Whether it's professional success, personal relationships, or self-actualization (be the

best you that you can be), committing to change empowers individuals to make progress and achieve their dreams.

6.   Making a Positive Impact: The commitment to lifelong change extends beyond personal growth and well-being; it also allows individuals to make a positive impact on their communities and the world at large. By continually striving to become better versions of ourselves, individuals become agents of change, inspiring and influencing others to follow suit. A single person's commitment to change can lead to a chain reaction, creating a more compassionate, just, fair, and sustainable world. My personal hope/goal/intent was to light this passion and fire in my own siblings, first and foremost. Selfish? Maybe. Maybe not. There are nine of us and if we can span out and offer our skills, talents, and knowledge across disciplines, industries, or areas of interest, I see this as all good.

7.   Unlocking Potential: Everyone possesses unique talents, abilities, and potential waiting to be unlocked. By committing to change, individuals actively explore and develop their strengths, allowing them to achieve their fullest potential. This commitment encourages individuals to step out of their comfort zones, pursue their passions, and contribute their unique gifts to the world, leading to a more meaningful and impactful existence. A prime example that I want to share is the need to surround yourself with those who have strengths that complement your weaknesses or areas where you can improve. Professor Deirdre Thompson has been that person for me for almost a decade now. Sometimes your fullest potential is unlocked when you share or team up with others—greatness is not typically achieved alone.

8.   Adaptation to a Changing World: Change is an inherent part of life, and the ability to embrace it is crucial for navigating an

ever-evolving world. By committing to lifelong change, individuals become more adaptable, flexible, and open-minded. They can easily adjust to new circumstances, embrace new technologies, and stay relevant in their personal and professional lives. A perfect example involves the seamless change from face-to-face teaching and learning to synchronous remote teaching and learning because of the global pandemic, COVID-19 and its many mutant strains that have evolved; this is an example of necessary change that occurred but is now a permanent need for some educators and learners for many reasons (i.e., health factors, personal factors such as the negative impact on childcare and women in the workforce, etc.). The next chapter is dedicated to moving the goal posts on purpose with purpose.

9. Leaving a Positive Legacy & Passing the Torch: Making a lifelong commitment to change for the better can have a lasting impact beyond one's own life. By actively working towards personal growth and positive change, individuals inspire and influence others around them. Through their example, they can motivate friends, family, and even future generations to pursue their own paths of personal development and contribute to a better world. The last chapter is dedicated to legacy building and torch passing.

10. Never Quit: Having a strong mindset of quitting not being an option is a necessity. Quitting is not an option for those who believe in themselves. The main takeaway is that all of this *requires you to believe in YOU.*

Making a lifelong commitment to change for the better is significant as it fosters continuous personal growth, enhances relationships, improves well-being, facilitates goal achievement, promotes adaptability, and leaves a positive legacy. By embracing change and actively working on self-improvement, individuals can lead more fulfilling lives and make a meaningful impact on themselves and those around them.

Our world is constantly evolving, and those who are resistant to change may struggle to adapt. Making a lifelong commitment to change equips individuals with the necessary skills and mindset to navigate through life's challenges effectively. This adaptability allows for a more successful response to unforeseen circumstances, new technologies, shifting social norms, and changing career landscapes. By remaining open to change, individuals can stay ahead of the curve and seize opportunities for personal and professional growth. Committing to personal change can have a ripple effect on others.

By leading through example, individuals inspire and motivate those around them to also embrace positive change. When others witness the growth and transformation that result from a lifelong commitment to change, they are encouraged to embark on their own journeys of self-improvement. This collective commitment to change can create a culture of growth, empathy, and support within families, communities, and organizations. In fact, making a lifelong commitment to change for the better not only benefits oneself but also contributes to the betterment of society. Positive change can lead to innovative solutions for societal issues, foster compassion and understanding, and drive progress. By actively working towards personal growth, individuals become better equipped to contribute their unique talents, skills, and perspectives to the world. Whether through volunteer work, entrepreneurship, advocacy, or leadership, their commitment to change can have a far-reaching impact on communities and help address pressing global challenges.

From the moment I made the decision to turn my life around— make a lifelong commitment to change—I knew it would not be easy.

I knew everything would not happen as I wanted it to when I wanted it to, but I also knew persistence and hard work turned working smarter would pay off. This chapter is intentionally short because the point is to have you reread and critically think about the ten points I have shared. Do not move on to the next chapter until you are ready because the next chapter is all about reminding you *there is no end game*.

PERSONAL LESSONS LEARNED

When I chose not to be a victim, I took the first step in fighting back fear and claiming my right to a healthy life. Then, when I chose to claim the belief that I was a survivor, I took the next all-important steps to fighting back fear. However, the greatest step of them all was when I realized I was more than simply a survivor because I thrived. I realized I am a servant leader!

I chose my own path in life. Despite doubters who thought I would never achieve greatness and would likely drop out of school as my parents did, I proved them all wrong. Not only did I graduate from high school at age 17 and join the military to escape the ghetto, but I also returned to school at age 30 and since have attained an associate degree, a bachelor's degree, a master's degree, and a doctoral degree. Despite naysayers who once said or thought I would end up pregnant as a young teen and eventually on public assistance, I proved them all wrong. Not only did I not have children young and before marriage, but I have now married my soulmate and plan to give my children, God-willing, all that I never had growing up. Despite dream-killers who don't believe in the business I have created I will flourish and still offer a hand of support in hopes that they will eventually believe they too can achieve greatness. Why am I saying this? It is not to brag. I want everyone who reads this book to take the challenges I present seriously. I want everyone who reads this to know they possess the power to create their own paths in life. I want everyone to know that I am passionate about helping people bring about change in their lives when they are ready to make a commitment to change. I am driven by my passion and my passion fuels my drive. Most importantly, I want everyone who reads this to understand their health matters, first and foremost because without a healthy you none of this will be possible. This means you must bring balance into your life mentally, emotionally, physically, and spiritually.

> "Knowing is not enough, we must apply.
> Willing is not enough, we must do."
> ~ Bruce Lee

MY CHALLENGE TO YOU

COMPLETE THE RESILIENCE TASK

The Resilience Theory framework posits that pointing out the strengths that people demonstrate enables them to rise above adversity and that in providing resources this will allow them to resolve their difficulties. Resilience is the ability of an individual to remain functionally stable in the face of stress or adversity and the ability to recover following a disturbance in their life. In other words, it is the capacity for an individual to be flexible and ready to bounce back after whatever life throws their way.

Occasionally, we experience a lack of balance in our lives. It could be that you are dissatisfied with your family and work, which is impacting you mentally and emotionally and perhaps even physically, as was the case for me. Yet, you have gained some level of momentum intellectually, socially, or spiritually, as was the case for me. Believe it or not this reflects resilience in action. I found a way to utilize the strengths I gained from other areas of my life to improve the adversity I was facing in other areas of my life. You can do the same! Complete the "Wheel of Health & Wellness Task" and think about how you have already been resilient whether you saw it that way before now.

The Wheel of Health & Wellness:

The eight sections in the Wheel of Health & Wellness represent how you see your current situation in life. Be honest with yourself in this task.

The titles currently labeled on the circle may not represent you in a meaningful way. If this is the case, draw a line through the current labels and replace them with a category that is meaningful to you. Then, rank your level of satisfaction within each of these categories in your life by drawing a line inside each area (0 is closest to the center representing no or very little satisfaction; 10 is the outer edge representing complete or a great deal of satisfaction). When you're done, look at the varying lines inside each area of the circle. What does your "Wheel of Health & Wellness" look like? Is it a rough ride or are you coming close to reaching all your goals?

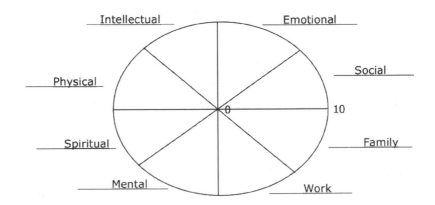

It appears from this example, that this person may be struggling mentally, emotionally, and intellectually, as well as with work and family. However, they seem to be satisfied with their spiritual, physical, and social areas of life. Perhaps, this is someone who meditates, works out, and surrounds themselves with family and friends who encourage them to keep pushing forward. The point is someone in this situation may be using the limited resources they have to keep striving for change. If they had someone to point this out to them, such as a role model, mentor, life coach or health and wellness coach, a challenge to gain control and turn things around is possible.

Now that you have completed your own "Wheel of Health & Wellness" take a moment to reflect on what yours looks like. Write down what you have visually depicted. Be honest with yourself. Then, briefly write how you can begin to address some of the areas you are dissatisfied with in your life if they exist. Before any goal posts can be moved, the first step requires belief in yourself and your readiness to make a lifelong commitment to change to realize the life you envision for yourself.

_____

_____

_____

_____

CHAPTER FOUR

MOVING THE GOAL POSTS ON PURPOSE WITH PURPOSE

Moving the Goal Posts on Purpose with Purpose

I n the pursuit of success, individuals often encounter unforeseen challenges, shifting circumstances, and evolving aspirations. To navigate this dynamic landscape, the concept of moving the goal posts on purpose with purpose emerges as a valuable and even necessary approach. While commonly associated with altering rules for personal advantage, when undertaken with integrity and intentionality, moving the goal posts becomes a powerful tool for personal or professional growth, adaptability, and the realization of one's true potential. This chapter explores the significance of embracing adaptability and intentionally redefining goals as a means of achieving success across the lifespan.

1. Embracing Adaptability as a Lifelong Learner: Life is a constant ebb and flow of change, and rigidly adhering to fixed goals can hinder progress. By intentionally moving the goal posts, individuals embrace adaptability and foster resilience in the face of shifting circumstances. This mindset allows for the

necessary adjustments to align objectives with newfound insights, changing environments, and emerging opportunities. The willingness to adapt demonstrates a proactive approach to success, empowering individuals to navigate challenges and seize new pathways.

2. Continuous Growth and Improvement: Moving the goal posts on purpose with purpose nurtures a mindset of continuous growth and improvement. Rather than perceiving success as a destination, individuals recognize it as an ongoing journey. As initial goals are achieved, new aspirations come to light. By intentionally raising the bar and redefining objectives, individuals challenge themselves to reach new levels of achievement, expand their capabilities, and unlock their full potential. This perpetual pursuit of improvement becomes a catalyst for personal growth, enabling individuals to evolve and thrive in all areas of life. Never place limitations on yourself.

3. Flexibility and Innovation: Intentionally moving the goal posts encourages flexibility and fosters innovation. When faced with obstacles or unforeseen challenges, individuals are empowered to reassess their objectives and find alternative pathways to obtain their goals. This adaptive mindset inspires innovative thinking, enabling individuals to explore creative solutions and challenge traditional approaches. By embracing this dynamic perspective, individuals cultivate the ability to navigate uncertainty, explore new limits, and find unconventional paths that lead to breakthrough achievements.

4. Expanding Possibilities: The deliberate act of moving the goal posts expands the realm of possibilities and opens doors or windows to new opportunities or adventures. By recognizing the limitations of initial objectives, individuals can broaden

their vision, aspire to greater heights, and dream bigger. This expansion of possibilities ignites a renewed sense of intrinsic motivation, enthusiasm, and passion. It pushes individuals beyond their comfort zones and encourages them to embrace calculated risks, facilitating personal and professional growth that transcends conventional boundaries. One thing about me for certain is that I am calculated; like it, love it, or hate it, it is part of who I am and have always been for as long as I can remember.

5. Fulfillment and Success: Moving the goal posts on purpose with purpose nurtures a sense of fulfillment and propels individuals towards true success and the pursuit of happiness, recognizing happiness is subjective. As individuals strive towards redefined goals aligned with their evolving aspirations, each milestone becomes a testament to personal growth and achievement. The iterative process of pushing boundaries, overcoming challenges, and embracing change instills a deep sense of satisfaction, bolstering self-confidence and reinforcing a positive mindset. This fulfillment arises not only from reaching destination points but also from the transformative journey undertaken in pursuit of success and happiness. This was the case for me as I worked toward earning my graduate and doctoral degrees and is now the case that I am creating my own journey of success in this one lifetime I get to live.

In the ever-changing landscape of life, the ability to adapt and redefine goals becomes paramount in the pursuit of success. Moving the goal posts on purpose with purpose offers a powerful strategy to navigate challenges, foster personal growth, and seize new opportunities. By embracing adaptability, continuous improvement, flexibility, and expansion of possibilities, individuals not only achieve their aspirations but also experience a sense of fulfillment and self-actualization. Through the deliberate act of moving the goal posts, individuals transcend limitations and embark on a transformative journey towards a successful and purposeful life. To be clear, self-actualization is *striving to be the best you that you can be in this lifetime.* If you are being true to you, keep moving the goal posts on purpose with purpose. Do what you must to stimulate your mind. Again, I will share another testament from my journey.

My journey in this life, thus far, has overflowed with challenges and accomplishments. I've had both disparaging and prideful moments that shaped me into the woman I am today. Grounded with faith the size of a mustard seed, I have worked diligently over the years to be an ethical and respectful, as well as respected person who will, going forward, learn the best of behavioral science to better our world, to shape the field, and to be the legacy I hope to pass on.

I have come to the realization that despite any odds, I can achieve my goals largely by working to control my own cognition, reasoning, and decision making. I can tell you that in this country and at this time, I am proof that it is still possible to defeat the odds and defy stereotypical claims about the limited capacities of minority ethnic and racial individuals. I exemplify the epitome of breaking barriers by overcoming adversity with hard work, perseverance, and pride.

I have been fortunate to gain research experience through summer internships and research assistantships during my undergraduate and master's level graduate years. To some degree, all my research experiences have advanced my knowledge and critical thinking of the vast psychological, biological, and social factors that shape or influence health functioning whether physical, mental, emotional, or social. The intersection of health behaviors and the permutation of those varying biopsychosocial factors are of particular interest to me and often guide the questions I hypothesize.

I believe it to be of extreme importance for future health psychologists, research professors, and advocates or organizational leaders of health promotion addressing health disparities among minority populations to explore, empirically test, and expand the knowledge base for critical analyses of such interactions. From experience and natural observation, I acknowledge individual experiences may vary greatly even when presented with seemingly similar circumstances, but it is the root of these differences that I am most interested in. Conducting research that aims to explore the interactions of biopsychosocial factors and health functioning among minority populations with hopes of reducing the health disparity gap is what led my decision to attain degrees in psychology with an emphasis in health behavior research, evaluation, and leadership. My doctoral degree is in organizational leadership with an emphasis on behavioral health research.

A foundation in health behavior research and evaluation has expanded my knowledge of health behavior theories combined with communication, social psychology, and program theories. However, I still have deep rooted personal questions about the perceived versus actual impact of psychological, biological, and social or environmental factors on health outcomes when considering minority populations given that the health disparity gap in our nation still has a way to go in reducing that gap. This book was developed to illustrate there are steps that must be taken to stimulate the mind and "power on" a commitment to change. It does not happen overnight. It won't magically occur simply because you wish it would. It will take real effort and dedication, but I promise you it is possible. Change is possible! Being who you dream to become is possible!

The mind is a powerful tool! If you begin to unlock the mysteries of just how powerful it is, you would be surprised by how far you may be willing to push yourself beyond your comfort zone. This was the case for me. It can be the case for you!

THE PERFECT TIME TO DO A GREAT THING

First, that is unrealistic. Is there really such a thing as "the perfect time" to do a great thing? I mean, really, life happens. If you are sitting around waiting for the perfect time to do something, you are committing spiritual suicide. Besides, when is the perfect time? The perfect time is when you create it. At the age of 30, in 2006, sitting in classrooms with many of the students ranging from age 18 to 20, it was no easy feat fighting back the lies of thinking I was too old to begin anew. I can laugh at that thought now, but it was not a laughing matter then. This is where support systems come into play and are lifelines. It may not have been the perfect time given I was having some major health issues and my family was displaced, but the sheer determination to do something about it *made it* the perfect time.

I wrote a poem a few years before this time, in 2003, that became my visual pusher. I had given a copy to my mom and all my siblings as well. I didn't find out until 10 years later that my sister, Kiarra, had used it as her visual pusher too. She told me she posted that poem above her bed in college. Then, she spun the camera around her master bedroom to show me that it was now above her dresser, after finishing college and working in her field as an elementary school teacher. My point is the perfect time to do something great is the moment you make that commitment to change or that commitment to achieve some goal or dream. I've decided to share that poem. It is titled "Strong Black Woman" and I wrote it in 2003 as a part of a collection of poems.

STRONG BLACK WOMAN

I'm a strong black woman standing unique unlike any other
And my strong right hand man is a unique black brother
The two of us forever
Will unite and survive together
The trial to conquer individuality has yet to end
So together we will contest with a new message to send
When I look in the mirror I am proud to see
A strong black woman, a woman of color, that is me
I will ascend to the top despite the effort it will take
Success by way of hard work is all that is at stake
With the right to stand by my belief in change
Society will hear me until equitable treatment is in range
So as a strong black woman, a woman of color
I will gather together my sisters and brothers
It is time that we learn the true importance of our past
And there it should stay, today united we shall steadfast
No matter how light to dark our skin or straight to kinky our hair
In this time of life the power to obtain knowledge
and move forward is equally fair
But to recognize this you must open your eyes
Welfare is a suppression, this you must realize
It's a way to hold you in a lower class known as unwilling to work
And as a strong black woman I refuse to be acknowledged as a jerk
In other words meaning: naïve, stupid or
insignificant to others around me
Wake up and take a long look at what I have learned to see
With a little effort and dedication
It's not hard to gain an education
And though there is nothing wrong with being a wonderful

housewife and mother
A Strong Black Woman is equally capable of holding the
positions said to be suited for a strong black brother
If I can see this, then so can you
Strong Black Woman you know what to do
Just as our ancestors did, hold your heads up high
And allow your expectations to exceed the sky
A doctor, lawyer, construction worker, whatever your dream or goal
Take the first step, put forth the effort and watch them all unfold
Because when I look in the mirror this is what I see
A Strong Black Woman, A Woman of Color, that is ME....

Victoria C. Johnson
©2003

I'll admit, I'm not in the realm of Maya Angelou or Nikki Giovani (two of my idols), but this poem meant a lot to me, and it inspired me to never give up on ME. However, what touched me more was the fact that I had positively affected my little sister in such a way that it too became her inspiration to never give up on HER goals and dreams. Inspiration can be found at any age and at any point in one's life. When I gave this poem to my sister, she couldn't have been more than 12 years old. Ten years later she still found inspiration in words I wrote that were honestly only meant to hold myself accountable. Getting back to there being a "perfect time", I hope that you are realizing that is a waste of time. My maternal grandmother used to always tell me that I should live my life like there is "no tomorrow" because the one thing you can never get back or rewind is time.

This notion of the "perfect time" was also proven wrong when I got to graduate school. I was no longer that student that was older than all my colleagues. In fact, the age range of students in graduate school is rather broad. There were students as young as 22 and as elderly as 70 in some of my classes. So, there you have it. Don't waste your time waiting for the "perfect time" to follow your dreams or attain goals that you're allowing doubt to hold you back from. Regardless to what some may say about school not being for everybody. Education creates a master key to success. However, knowledge alone is not as powerful as the wisdom to use it in a manner that is beneficial.

Finally, I want to point out that I'm not suggesting you can't be successful without degrees. I'm simply saying that if you're in a position that you know is not where you want to be then you should weigh all your options and take the best route for you. If that happens to be school, then give it all you got and don't worry about how late you got in the game. What will matter is that you're in the game and what will determine whether you will win is solely up to the effort you put into it.

PAYING IT FORWARD

As a mentor and an academic coach, it has been my pleasure to help others reach their fullest potential. I do not claim to know everything, but what I have done in instances when I was not certain is research the resources that are available. I have made it my business to develop a networking circle that encompasses a range of people with varying levels of expertise. This has helped me personally and has served as a platform of help when I needed to refer someone to someone else with more in-depth knowledge or understanding of a particular subject. It is personally satisfying to help someone else attain their goals. This has especially been the case when that person has demonstrated they are hungry for success.

I pointed out there were steps that had to be taken to take such a journey. I hope to pay it forward by continuing to instill that it is never too late. Having an education and pushing the mind beyond boundaries you may believe exist is powerful. However, there was a quote inserted in the past chapter that is necessary to understand. Simply because one possesses knowledge does not make them powerful. It is what they do with that knowledge that makes them powerful.

The only thing, aside from death, that will be able to stop me, is me. This does not suggest setbacks will not occur, but here is where the steps come into play. It takes planning to achieve almost anything. The first step in the plan is to prepare the mind for a commitment to change. This is the most critical step and is the step that will help you through any obstacles that may come your way. You may face financial problems, family loss, health issues, and a host of other life occurrences that may seem to slow you down. There are positive situations that can possibly slow you down. For instance, you may decide to get married and start a family. The difference is this. It's nothing wrong with having to slow down. It is when you stop and give up that defeat has won. The next critical step is establishing discipline. This tends to be the most difficult step for some, especially those who have allowed their circumstances to dictate and guide them in life. You must prepare the mind and establish discipline before a commitment to change can take form. These are the challenges I help my clients with during coaching sessions because I know it sometimes takes a combination of intrinsic and extrinsic motivation as well as inspiration from someone who has done it.

I have always led my mission to pay it forward by pushing those closest to me. I encourage my family and friends to go as far as their heart's desire when it comes to getting an education and better positioning themselves in life and in this society. It is not a secret that the more education one has the better they can position themselves in the workforce. The better you position yourself in the workforce the more you can do for you and your family unit. The more you can do for you and your family unit the further distance you can place between you all and the hardships that result from poverty. These steps are not the easiest to conquer, but they are possible to conquer!

Ultimately, I will continue to do my part to pay it forward by continuing to push as many people as possible in the direction of making life better for them. This includes intellectually, emotionally, mentally, physically, and spiritually. This is the legacy I intend to leave behind—one of promoting health and wellness, success, and prosperity.

MY CHALLENGE TO YOU

WRITE AN EFFECTIVE PERSONAL STATEMENT

Most colleges, whether a community college or a four-year institution, require that you write an effective personal statement as a part of the application process. I find that writing a strong personal statement makes one think deeply about who they are, what they've been through in life—challenges and successes, what they want out of life, and what it will truly take to make their dreams a reality. People do this when they write a cover letter to attach with a job application. The purpose is to inform and persuade tactfully. My challenge to you is to take the necessary time to sit down and write an effective personal statement meant to persuade *you* that you are ready for the next chapter in your life—the one you are about to write.

Some Tips:
Be Honest
Be Direct
Be Creative
Be Confident
Be Tactful
Be Persuasive

Most importantly, get someone to read it and critique it for you. You must be open to constructive criticism and be prepared to change/adapt if necessary.

CHAPTER FIVE

LEGACY BUILDING
AND
TORCH PASSING

Legacy Building and Torch Passing

Leadership is a profound responsibility that goes beyond personal or professional success. Successful servant leaders not only strive for their own achievements but also focus on building a legacy and passing the torch to the next generation of leaders. Legacy building involves creating a lasting impact and imprint on society, while torch passing ensures the continuity of progress and the development of future leaders. This chapter explores the significance of legacy building and torch passing as essential qualities of a successful leader in society. An introduction to both topics is presented first. Then, each topic will be delved into more in-depth.

1. Leaving a Positive Impact on Society: A successful and effective servant leader aims to leave a lasting, positive impact on society. This could be achieved through initiatives that address social, economic, or environmental challenges. By creating sustainable solutions, servant leaders can improve the lives of individuals and communities, leaving behind a legacy of

progress and improvement. A servant leader's legacy inspires and motivates future generations to continue the work they started. By setting an example of determination, integrity, and empathy, servant leaders cultivate a culture of excellence and encourage others to strive for greatness. Servant leaders with strong values and ethical principles instill these virtues in the organizations and communities they serve. By fostering a culture of integrity, servant leaders ensure that their legacy transcends their own tenure and becomes an inherent part of the collective consciousness.

2. Torch Passing by Mentoring and Nurturing Future Talent: Successful servant leaders recognize the importance of nurturing and developing emerging talent. By mentoring aspiring leaders, they equip them with the necessary skills, knowledge, and experience to take on future challenges. Through mentorship, coaching, guidance, and support, they ensure a smooth transition of leadership and enable the growth of the next generation. A successful servant leader empowers others by delegating responsibilities and encouraging autonomous decision-making. By entrusting capable individuals with significant tasks, they create opportunities for growth and development, fostering a sense of ownership and accountability. Effective servant leaders understand the importance of succession planning. They actively identify potential successors and groom them for leadership roles. By investing in the next generation of leaders, they ensure the continuity of their vision and work, maintaining stability and progress within organizations and communities.

Legacy building and torch passing are indispensable components of successful leadership in society. By focusing not only on personal and professional achievements but also on the long-term impact and development of future leaders, a servant leader can leave behind a respectable legacy. Through their actions and values, they inspire others and instill a sense of purpose, ensuring that their work continues beyond their own time. As society evolves, it is the responsibility of successful servant leaders to build a strong legacy and pass the torch, paving the way for a brighter future—reminding those gems in the rough, all along the way, that they soon will be ready to be transformed into the priceless diamonds they are and will shine ever so brightly in the future.

Leaving behind a positive impact requires due diligence during your charge. As servant leaders, the desire to leave behind a positive impact is a noble aspiration. However, building a legacy necessitates due diligence and conscientious efforts during your time in charge. Simply aiming for a positive impact is not enough; it is the responsibility of servant leaders to ensure that their actions, decisions, and policies are carefully executed to maximize the potential for creating a beneficial and sustainable impact. This section delves into the importance of due diligence in leadership and how it contributes to leaving a positive legacy.

1. Ethical decision-making:
    a. Consideration of stakeholders: Successful leaders exercise due diligence by considering the interests and well-being of all stakeholders affected by their decisions. This includes employees, customers, shareholders, communities, and the environment. By thoroughly assessing the potential consequences of their choices, servant leaders can make informed decisions that align with ethical principles and promote positive outcomes for all.
    b. Long-term perspective: Leaders should adopt a long-term perspective rather than focusing solely on short-term

gains. They must evaluate the potential impact of their decisions on future generations and the sustainability of their initiatives. By incorporating foresight into their decision-making, effective servant leaders can ensure that their actions have a lasting and positive effect on society.

2. Strategic planning and implementation:
    a. Thorough research and analysis: Servant leaders who exercise due diligence invest time and effort into conducting comprehensive research and analysis. They gather relevant data, seek expert opinions, and consider various perspectives to make well-informed strategic plans. By basing their decisions on accurate information, servant leaders can mitigate risks and increase the likelihood of achieving positive outcomes for all.
    b. Implementation monitoring: Successful servant leaders actively monitor the implementation of their plans and policies. They assess progress, identify potential obstacles, and adjust when necessary. Through diligent oversight, effective servant leaders can ensure that their initiatives remain on track and are effectively executed, maximizing the potential for positive impact.

3. Continuous improvement and learning:
    a. Reflection and evaluation: Servant leaders committed to leaving a positive impact engage in regular reflection and evaluation of their actions and outcomes. They identify areas for improvement, acknowledge mistakes, and actively seek feedback from their family, friends, colleagues, peers, and other stakeholders such as those aspired by their leadership (e.g., mentees, students/

learners, constituents, etc.). By embracing a growth mindset, servant leaders can adapt their approaches, rectify shortcomings, and continuously enhance their effectiveness in creating positive change.

b. Learning from past leaders: Studying the legacies of past leaders, both their successes and failures, is crucial for due diligence. By understanding historical precedents, effective servant leaders can learn valuable lessons and avoid repeating past mistakes. Learning from the experiences of others allows servant leaders to refine their strategies and ensure a more impactful and sustainable legacy.

Leaving behind a positive impact as a servant leader requires meticulous due diligence during your charge. Ethical decision-making, strategic planning, implementation monitoring, and continuous improvement are essential components of this process. By exercising due diligence, servant leaders maximize their potential to create positive and lasting change. Ultimately, the dedication to thoroughness and conscientiousness throughout their tenure sets the stage for a legacy that truly makes a difference in society.

Passing the torch to the next generation is a crucial responsibility of successful servant leaders. To ensure the growth and development of future talent, servant leaders must engage in mentoring and nurturing initiatives. This involves knowledge sharing, skills development, networking opportunities, and fostering a "no quit" attitude through accountability and a paying it forward mindset (Taylor, 2022). Servant leaders create "living purple prints" that can be passed on, adapted, improved on, and ultimately added to as it becomes the framework for the next generation. This section explores the significance of these elements in effective torch passing and the long-term impact they have on the success of future leaders.

1. Knowledge Sharing:
   a. Transfer of expertise: Successful and effective servant leaders have accumulated valuable knowledge and experiences throughout their careers. By actively sharing this expertise with emerging talent, they equip them with practical insights and wisdom. This transfer of knowledge helps future leaders navigate challenges, make informed decisions, and avoid common pitfalls.
   b. Open communication: Servant leaders foster an environment of open communication where knowledge is freely shared. They encourage dialogue, actively listen to diverse perspectives, and engage in discussions that encourage critical thinking and innovation. Through these interactions, servant leaders create a culture of continuous learning and knowledge exchange.

2. Skills Development:
   a. Identifying potential: Effective servant leaders identify the unique strengths and talents of future leaders and provide opportunities for skills development in those areas. By investing in their growth, servant leaders enable individuals to reach their full potential, equipping them with the necessary skills and competencies to excel in their respective fields.
   b. Encouraging continuous learning: Servant leaders promote a culture of continuous learning and personal growth. They provide resources, such as training programs, workshops, and educational opportunities, to enhance the skill sets of aspiring leaders. By encouraging self-improvement, leaders cultivate a mindset of lifelong learning, ensuring the continuous development of talent.

3. Networking Opportunities:
    a. Building connections: Successful servant leaders recognize the importance of networking and building relationships. They facilitate opportunities for future leaders to connect with industry professionals, experts, and mentors who can offer guidance, support, and valuable insights. Through networking, emerging talent gains access to diverse perspectives, career opportunities, and collaborative partnerships.
    b. Creating a supportive community: Servant leaders foster a sense of community and collaboration among future leaders. By organizing events, forums, and mentorship programs, they facilitate peer-to-peer learning and the exchange of ideas. This supportive environment encourages the growth of a strong network that benefits both individuals and the broader community.

4. "No Quit" Attitude:
    a. Cultivating accountability: Successful servant leaders instill a sense of accountability in future leaders. They encourage individuals to take ownership of their actions, learn from failures, and persist in the face of challenges. By fostering a "no quit" attitude, servant leaders empower emerging talent to overcome obstacles and persevere on their path to success.
    b. Paying it forward: Servant leaders encourage future leaders to embrace a paying it forward mindset. By witnessing the support and mentorship they received, emerging talent is inspired to give back to others who are just starting their journeys. This creates a cycle of continuous mentorship, coaching, guidance, and support, ensuring the sustained growth and development of future leaders.

Torch passing through mentoring and nurturing future talent requires knowledge sharing, skills development, networking opportunities, and a "no quit" attitude. By actively engaging in these initiatives, successful and effective servant leaders ensure that the next generation is well-prepared to take on leadership roles and make a positive impact. Aspiring leaders benefit from the wisdom and experiences of their mentors, develop essential skills, build valuable connections, and cultivate resilience. Ultimately, the successful passing of the torch paves the way for a strong and sustainable leadership legacy that transcends individual contributions and positively shapes society.

One final circle back, to demonstrate the connection to a lifelong commitment to change, beginning with the end in mind: it likely will not be easy, the journey may take on shifting pathways, there may be a plethora of "no responses" before you get the first "yes response" that could change your life for the better, potentially forever, and take serious your own role, actions, thoughts, decisions, and emotions because you are the future! Everyone is watching. Welcome it, and then, shine gem in the rough.

REFERENCES

Taylor, V. C. (2022). *Qualitative Descriptive Investigation: Minority Transfer Students' Mentoring Experiences in an Entrepreneurship Program* (Order No. 29322960). Available from ProQuest Central. (2711011947). https://ezproxy.pgcc.cdu/login?url=https://www.pro-quest.com/dissertations-theses/qualitative-descriptive-investigation-minority/docview/2711011947/se-2

Printed in the United States
by Baker & Taylor Publisher Services